SHORT WALKS
FOREST OF DEAN

by Mike Dunn

Outstanding woodland walking at Horse Lea (Walk 6)

CONTENTS

Using this guide...4
Route summary table...6
Map key...7
Introduction..9
  Walking in the Forest of Dean......................................9
  Special things to see...10
  Bases and places to stay..11
  Travel..11

The walks

1.	Tidenham Chase and the Devil's Pulpit	13
2.	The Hudnalls and the Wye	17
3.	Redbrook and Newland	23
4.	The Kymin from Wyesham	29
5.	Near Hearkening Rock and the Buckstone	35
6.	Brierley and Ruardean Hill	41
7.	Bixslade and Cannop	47
8.	The Dean Sculpture Trail	53
9.	Nagshead Nature Reserve	57
10.	Crabtree Hill and Woorgreens Lake	63
11.	Soudley Valley Rural Geology Trail	67
12.	Blaize Bailey from Soudley Ponds	71
13.	May Hill	77
14.	St Anthony's Well and Welshbury Hill	83
15.	Newnham and Haie Hill	89

Useful information..95

USING THIS GUIDE

Routes in this book

In this book you will find a selection of easy or moderate walks suitable for almost everyone, including casual walkers and families with children, or for when you only have a short time to fill. The routes have been carefully chosen to allow you to explore the area and its attractions. Most routes are circular or out-and-back, although some linear walks may be included that use public transport to get back to the start. Although there may be some climbs there is no challenging terrain, but do bear in mind that conditions can sometimes be wet or muddy underfoot. A route summary table is included on page 6 to help you choose the right walk.

Clothing and footwear

You won't need any special equipment to enjoy these walks. The weather in Britain can be changeable, so choose clothing suitable for the season and wear or carry a waterproof jacket. For footwear, comfortable walking boots or trainers with a good grip are best. A small rucksack for drinks, snacks and spare clothing is useful. See www.adventuresmart.uk.

Walk descriptions

At the beginning of each walk you'll find all the information you need:

- start/finish location, with a what3words address to help you find it
- parking and transport information, estimated walking time, total distance and climb
- details of public toilets available along the route and where you can get refreshments
- a summary of the key highlights of the walk and what you might see

Timings given are the time to complete the walk at a reasonable walking pace. Allow extra time for extended stops or if walking with children.

The route is described in clear, easy-to-follow directions, with each waypoint marked on an accompanying map extract. It's a good idea to read the whole of the route instructions before setting out, so that you know what to expect.

Maps, GPX files and what3words

Extracts from the OS® 1:25,000 map accompany each route. GPX files for all the walks in this book are available to download at www.cicerone.co.uk/1288/gpx.

What3words is a free smartphone app which identifies every 3m square of the globe with a unique three-word address, e.g. ///destiny.cafe.sonic. For more information see https://what3words.com/products/what3words-app.

USING THIS GUIDE

Walking with children

Even young children can be surprisingly strong walkers, but every family is different and you may need to adapt the timings given in this book to take that into account. Make sure you go at the pace of the slowest member and choose a walk with an exciting objective in mind, such as a cave, river, waterfall or picnic spot. Many of the walks can be shortened to suit – suggestions are included at the end of the route description.

Dogs

Sheep or cattle may be found grazing on a number of these walks. Keep dogs under control at all times so that they don't scare or disturb livestock or wildlife. Cattle, particularly cows with calves, may very occasionally pose a risk to walkers with dogs. If you ever feel threatened by cattle, you should let go of your dog's lead and let it run free.

Enjoying the countryside responsibly

Enjoy the countryside and treat it with respect to protect our natural environments. Stick to footpaths and take your litter home with you. When driving, slow down on rural roads and park considerately, or better still use public transport. For more details check out www.gov.uk/countryside-code.

The Countryside Code

Respect everyone
- be considerate to those living in, working in and enjoying the countryside
- leave gates and property as you find them
- do not block access to gateways or driveways when parking
- be nice, say hello, share the space
- follow local signs and keep to marked paths unless wider access is available

Protect the environment
- take your litter home – leave no trace of your visit
- do not light fires and only have BBQs where signs say you can
- always keep dogs under control and in sight
- dog poo – bag it and bin it – any public waste bin will do
- care for nature – do not cause damage or disturbance

Enjoy the outdoors
- check your route and local conditions
- plan your adventure – know what to expect and what you can do
- enjoy your visit, have fun, make a memory

ROUTE SUMMARY TABLE

WALK NAME	START POINT	TIME	DISTANCE
1. Tidenham Chase and the Devil's Pulpit	Tidenham Chase	1hr 45min	6.2km (3.9 miles)
2. The Hudnalls and the Wye	Brockweir Bridge	2hr 45min	8.1km (5 miles)
3. Redbrook and Newland	Redbrook Village Hall	2hr 30min	7.3km (4.5 miles)
4. The Kymin from Wyesham	St James' Church, Wyesham	1hr 45min	5.5km (3.4 miles)
5. Near Hearkening Rock and the Buckstone	White Horse pub, Staunton	2hr 30min	7.3km (4.5 miles)
6. Brierley and Ruardean Hill	Brierley	2hr 30min	7.7km (4.8 miles)
7. Bixslade and Cannop	Cannop Ponds	3hr	9.4km (5.8 miles)
8. The Dean Sculpture Trail	Beechenhurst Lodge	2hr	6.8km (4.2 miles)
9. Nagshead Nature Reserve	Nagshead visitor centre	1hr 45min	6km (3.7 miles)
10. Crabtree Hill and Woorgreens Lake	Speech House Woodlands	1hr 30min	4.5km (2.8 miles)
11. Soudley Valley Rural Geology Trail	Soudley Village Hall	1hr 30min	4.4km (2.7 miles)
12. Blaize Bailey from Soudley Ponds	Soudley Ponds	1hr 45min	4.7km (2.9 miles)
13. May Hill	Glasshouse	3hr	8km (5 miles)
14. St Anthony's Well and Welshbury Hill	Gunn's Mill	1hr 45min	5.3km (3.3 miles)
15. Newnham and Haie Hill	Newnham High Street	2hr 30min	8.6km (5.3 miles)

ROUTE SUMMARY TABLE

HIGHLIGHTS
Offa's Dyke, Tintern Abbey view
Offa's Dyke Path, Wye gorge
Cathedral of the Forest
Kymin parkland, Round House
Autumn colours, rock scenery
Beaver enclosure, industrial relics
Tramroads, freemines, scenic lakes
Art in the Forest
Birdwatching, historic ironworks
Restored heathland
Rock exposures, ancient quarries
Superb viewpoint, heritage centre
Iconic summit
Ancient healing well, hill fort
Historic railway tunnel, old river port

SYMBOLS USED ON ROUTE MAPS

 Start point

 Finish point

 Start and finish at the same place

 Waypoint

~ Route line

MAPPING IS SHOWN AT A SCALE OF 1:25,000

0 KM   0.25   0.5
0 miles   0.25

DOWNLOAD THE GPX FILES FOR FREE AT
www.cicerone.co.uk/1288/gpx

The track to Miss Grace's Lane (Walk 1)

INTRODUCTION

The Wye Valley from Readings (Walk 6)

According to the playwright Dennis Potter, who was born there, the Forest of Dean is as beautiful as any place on earth. An exaggeration, perhaps, but this idiosyncratic, otherworldly place has that effect, with a surprise around every corner, whether it's a stunning view or a glimpse of fallow deer or, even more exotically, wild boar. Hemmed in by rivers and hidden by encircling ridges, richly wooded and heavily dissected by fast-flowing streams, the central forest is enchanting: landscape and people are deeply intertwined, the colours – especially in autumn – are extraordinary, and the walking is varied, none too challenging and above all richly rewarding.

Walking in the Forest of Dean

Despite its compact size, sandwiched between the Severn and the Wye, the Forest of Dean offers a magical blend of outstanding scenery, industrial history and richly varied wildlife. It is very much a walker's paradise, with a plethora of paths, tracks and forest roads providing endless possibilities. There are almost too many options – but the signposting is generally good, the selected routes are easy to follow and all the walks are circular.

Ancient trackways and Roman roads are thin on the ground, but it's a delight to follow medieval routes such as French Lane near Redbrook

The distinctive summit of May Hill (Walk 13)

or discover abandoned turnpike roads such as Wyegate Lane, now reduced to a stony track but still offering a memorable experience. Elsewhere walkers can make use of old tramroads, their stone sleeper blocks still in place.

A superb network of accessible shared paths criss-crosses the Forest, largely based on the dense network of old railway lines which originally served mines and quarries but have now been reimagined as modern off-road routes for cyclists and walkers.

Special things to see

The spectacular gorge of the lower Wye Valley on the western fringe of Dean inspired early lovers of picturesque scenery, many of whom took the 'Wye tour' in the later 18th century, and today the area's rich mosaic of special landscapes still holds rich rewards, from the stunning autumn displays of colour in the deciduous woodlands to open heathlands such as Crabtree Hill. Renowned viewpoints include the view of Tintern Abbey from the Devil's Pulpit (Walk 1), Blaize Bailey overlooking the Severn meanders (Walk 12) and May Hill with its 360-degree panorama (Walk 13).

The Forest was at the forefront of innovation as the industrial revolution gathered pace, and substantial remains of ironworks, forges, furnaces and millponds can be visited today at Whitecliff, Dark Hill (where modern steel was invented), Gunn's Mill and elsewhere. Industry has left indelible marks in different ways, from the deeply gouged hollows known as scowles created by a combination of erosion and early iron mining, to the small-scale freemines worked by locally born coalminers. Just as important are the remains of the tramroads and early railways which transported forest products to ports on the River Severn.

The wildlife of Dean is impressive, with the largest population of wild boar in Britain now roaming the woodlands and a growing number of goshawks careering through the trees in search of prey. Herds of fallow deer can be glimpsed in the woods, while other notable birds include mandarin ducks, which breed on some of the larger lakes, and nightjars, whose distinctive churring call enlivens summer evenings on the heaths.

A host of visitor attractions provides further incentive to prolong a visit to the Forest. The Dean Forest Railway runs between Lydney and Parkend, while at Puzzlewood visitors can enjoy contorted rock formations. The impressive caverns at Clearwell Caves, where iron ore was mined in the Bronze Age, and the excellent sculpture trail at Beechenhurst (which also has a cafe, playground and treetop adventure course) provide memorable experiences.

Wild boar at Beechenhurst (Walk 8)

Autumn above Near Hearkening Rock (Walk 5)

Bases and places to stay

The Forest is ringed by towns with a variety of options for accommodation, including Chepstow, Monmouth, Lydney and Gloucester, while within the area there are country house hotels, village inns, self-catering properties, and sites with woodland lodges and camping facilities.

Travel

The M4, M5, M48 and M50 motorways all provide easy access to the Forest of Dean, and regular train services on the Birmingham to Cardiff route call at Gloucester, Lydney and Chepstow. Buses from all these locations serve many of the towns and villages in the Forest and the lower Wye Valley, and the majority of the walks in this book can easily be accessed from one of these services.

The Jubilee Stone on Parson's Allotment

WALK 1
Tidenham Chase and the Devil's Pulpit

Start/finish	Tidenham Chase
Locate	///verge.sung.sinkhole
Cafes/pubs	None on route
Transport	No public transport
Parking	Tidenham Chase car park, signposted for Offa's Dyke (NP16 7JN)
Toilets	No public toilets on route

Time 1hr 45min
Distance 6.2km (3.9 miles)
Climb 120m

Wonderful open heathland, Offa's Dyke and the classic view of Tintern Abbey

This is an easy and relatively short walk which includes spectacular stretches of the Saxon earthwork of Offa's Dyke, with a remarkable view of Tintern Abbey. The route crosses the heathland of Tidenham Chase, which is now being actively managed, using Exmoor ponies for grazing, to improve the habitat by restoring native woodland and clearing plantations to increase the area of sandy heath.

The entrance to The Park

SHORT WALKS FOREST OF DEAN

1 Walk past the Forestry England sign for **The Park**, taking the obvious track across the open heath of Tidenham Chase. The Chase is the most significant fragment of lowland heathland to survive in Gloucestershire. Pass a trig point and go through a wooden kissing gate onto a clear track as far as **Miss Grace's Lane**, originally a prehistoric trackway.

2 Go left and immediately right across the lane, onto a track signposted to Offa's Dyke Path and the Devil's Pulpit. An easy walk now crosses four fields, enters woodland again and immediately arrives at Offa's Dyke Path; 50m to the left is the **Devil's Pulpit**, an extraordinary clifftop lookout.

The Devil's Pulpit, a spectacular rock stack above the cliff face, has sensational views of Tintern Abbey, built by the Cistercians in the 13th century. The devil supposedly tempted the monks from his vantage point here.

3 The route now lies south, along one of the best preserved sections of Offa's Dyke, with earthen ramparts up to 6m high. Follow the path as it contours above the great limestone face of **Plumweir Cliff**. The trees have been felled in places to reveal views of the Wye and Tintern Abbey. The route used to lie along the top of the earthwork, but a new path has been constructed alongside to preserve the

Tintern Abbey from the Devil's Pulpit

Dyke. Turn left onto a wide track, and when Offa's Dyke Path swings away to the right, take the roughly surfaced lane past cottages to the **B4228**.

4 Turn right along the road for 150m, find the footpath sign on the left and go through a kissing gate onto a good path through **Parson's Allotment**. Keep ahead at a crossroads of paths, then bear right and sharply left, now following the Gloucestershire Way northwards as far as a minor lane. Just to the right is the Jubilee Stone, erected in 1897 to mark Queen Victoria's platinum jubilee.

Classic lowland heath on Poor's Allotment

5 Turn left along the lane, then take the path on the right to cross **Poor's Allotment**, an open area with rough grassland, patches of gorse and bracken, and one or two copses. A delightful grassy path leads straight ahead, with the view on the right particularly impressive. Turn left at an obvious crossroads of paths in the middle of Poor's Allotment, heading slightly uphill towards the thin belt of woodland known as **Beacon Ash**, and follow the clear path which leads to an ornate gate and, across the B4228, the Tidenham Chase car park.

Poor's Allotment was created for the benefit of the needy (Parson's Allotment, though, was given to the vicar). The land was originally divided into animal pasture, a potato garden and allotments.

+ To lengthen

Turn right at Waypoint 2, take Miss Grace's Lane to join Offa's Dyke Path by Beeches Farm and follow this to Waypoint 3, adding 2.5km (45min).

WALK 2
The Hudnalls and the Wye

Start/finish	Brockweir Bridge
Locate	///clipboard.electrode.sponsors
Cafes/pubs	None on route. Cafe at Old Station, Tintern (400m south of bridge)
Transport	Bus 69 (hourly) from Chepstow to Brockweir Bridge
Parking	Roadside parking in Brockweir
Toilets	At Old Station, Tintern (400m south of bridge)

Time 2hr 45min
Distance 8.1km (5 miles)
Climb 280m

A climb on Offa's Dyke Path, the intricate landscape of the Hudnalls and easy riverside walking along the Wye

A walk of huge contrasts, starting with the historic and attractive village of Brockweir, and then the distinctive and secluded area of the Hudnalls, with its narrow lanes, minuscule fields and squatter's cottages. A descent to the well-wooded gorge of the River Wye follows, tracing the course of the picturesque Wye Tour and passing one of the many weirs controlled by the monks of Tintern Abbey further downstream.

Brockweir's Moravian chapel, with Caswell Wood and Madgett's Hill beyond

SHORT WALKS FOREST OF DEAN

1 Start at the bridge over the Wye and walk through the hamlet of **Brockweir**, passing the (closed) pub and turning right by the medieval Malt House, with its adjacent Monks Hall. Turn left (signposted with an Offa's Dyke Path acorn waymark) onto a stony track after about 100m. Climb steadily on the track, passing through a gate, before turning left at a signpost (waymarked as the higher route through the Hudnalls).

> A former river port, Brockweir had a wharf used by Severn trows taking goods down the River Wye. There were once a dozen inns, and there is still a Moravian chapel alongside a Gothic manse and gabled Sunday school.

2 Drop down on a green path to cross a stream, climb up to cross a road and take a restricted byway over a stream to another lane at **Rock Farm**. Go slightly left onto a green lane, still following Offa's Dyke Path as it climbs steadily and continues straight ahead at a crossroads, now on a gravelly path between hedges, to reach a road near **Hill Farm**.

3 Turn left and follow the road for 300m before branching off to the right, passing an old chapel to

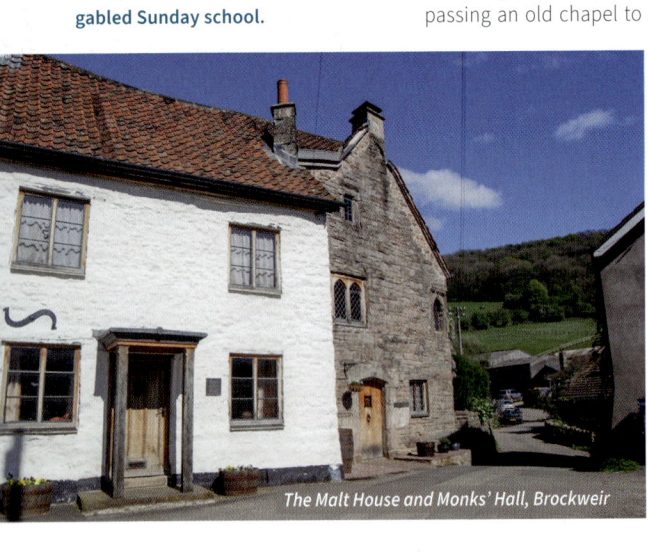

The Malt House and Monks' Hall, Brockweir

find an ancient walled lane traversing **St Briavels Common**. Still going gently uphill, turn left at a junction of paths and briefly left again onto a lane before turning right. Go through a gate and pass a colourful corrugated iron hut, keeping to the right-hand field edge before reaching another of the narrow, twisting lanes characteristic of the **Hudnalls**.

4 Turn right along the lane, follow it around a couple of sharp bends and then leave it to the left on a track

Llandogo seen across the River Wye

The descent towards Woodside House

running between tall hedges. Turn right onto a lane and then left after 200m over a stone stile onto a signposted path.

5 The path, through a copse at first, is well marked as it negotiates two more stiles before reaching a tarmac lane. Turn left here and keep straight on as it becomes a ridged concrete track descending quite steeply. Go straight on past Blue Barn, then fork right onto a delightful signposted path through the trees. Keep straight on at the woodland edge to go across a green track, with **Woodside House** on the right. A good path leads across another green track and down to meet a bridleway, with the village of Llandogo now clearly in view ahead.

WALK 2 – THE HUDNALLS AND THE WYE

6 Turn left along the bridleway, which runs through sheep pastures and gradually approaches the River Wye. The easy riverside path runs beneath trees for a while, with **Coed-Ithel weir** down to the right. Known as Ithelwere in 1334, Coed-Ithel was owned by Tintern Abbey, who controlled the fishing rights along the river in medieval times. The path then traverses narrow riverside fields and passes a boathouse before approaching the remains of the quay in the shadow of **Brockweir Bridge**.

> ⓘ *Offa's Dyke Path runs for 285km (177 miles) between Chepstow and Prestatyn, with some of its most dramatic stretches above the lower Wye Valley.*

The Hudnalls

The Hudnalls from the south

The Hudnalls were once an area of common wood-pasture and a detached part of the Forest of Dean. This special landscape hidden away above the Wye owes its character to its colonisation by squatters in the late 18th century. Narrow lanes and secret paths divide tiny fields carpeted by wildflowers such as sheep's sorrel in spring and early summer. Millstones were once quarried in the Hudnalls and rolled down the hillside to be loaded into barges on the river.

Birt's Cottage below Highbury Wood

WALK 3
Redbrook and Newland

Time 2hr 30min
Distance 7.3km (4.5 miles)
Climb 150m

Start/finish	Redbrook Village Hall
Locate	///stooping.smooth.handover
Cafes/pubs	Cafe and pubs in Redbrook, pub in Newland
Transport	Bus 69 (hourly) from Chepstow to Redbrook
Parking	Two car parks in Redbrook (NP25 4ND)
Toilets	In Newland church

A climb through woodland, a magnificent church, then lanes and tracks around a dramatic abandoned river meander

Although this is a short walk it is packed full of interest, from the initial climb up medieval French Lane to the spectacular village church in Newland, and the delightful walk around the former course of the River Wye, now an abandoned meander traversed by a misfit stream too small to have created the present valley. The return to Redbrook passes former furnace ponds, the site of copper smelting and tinplate works and a riverside wharf.

The path to Newland

1 Start with the village hall on the right and the primary school on the left and climb, steeply at first, on French Lane. Known as French Way by 1422, this lane provided the most direct route between Redbrook and Newland. The slope eases as the tarmac ends and a stony track provides a superb walk through **Forge Wood**. A forest ride joins from the left and the route levels out, becoming somewhat muddy at times, before rising gently to a complex junction at the ridge top, with superb and wide-ranging views to the north and east.

2 Go through a gate onto a green lane, then turn immediately left onto a well-signposted footpath which descends through a succession of fields, with the tower of Newland church and Bircham Wood framing the view ahead. Go straight ahead past **Greenbank Farm** onto Laundry Lane, then climb steep Savage Hill to emerge in the lovely village of **Newland** at the corner of the massive churchyard. There are almshouses to the right and the venerable Ostrich Inn straight ahead.

Newland church, the Cathedral of the Forest

WALK 3 – REDBROOK AND NEWLAND

3 Return to Laundry Lane and swing left onto the quiet lane leading past pheasant pens and evidence of deer stalking towards **Lodges Farm**. The lane traces the course of an abandoned meander of the River Wye, eventually crossing the **Valley Brook** on a substantial bridge just below the farm.

Valley Brook occupying an abandoned meander of the Wye

The extinct meander at Newland is around 115m above the current river level, indicating the powerful forces in the last Ice Age which enabled the Wye to straighten its course by cutting through the neck of the meander.

4 Fork right just below Lodges Farm onto a green lane (signposted as a restricted byway), which curves round the core of the meander at some distance above the current misfit stream.

The scenery here is superb, with Highbury Wood and Astridge Wood framing the green fields in the valley. The route passes **Birt's Cottage** (a rebuilding of a 17th-century house)

> ⓘ *The Normans stamped their authority on Dean by building a ring of major churches around the Forest, at Ruardean, Mitcheldean, Newland and elsewhere.*

WALK 3 – REDBROOK AND NEWLAND

and, after passing ponds marking the course of the meander, reaches a junction of paths near Glyn Farm.

5 Take the path to the right, ignoring the bridleway on its left, and walk between the stream on the left and deciduous woodland on the right to pass three ponds. These furnace ponds supplied the tinplate and copper works in Lower Redbrook, which operated from the late 17th century until the 1960s. The path becomes a back lane for suburban housing; look out for a substantial series of concrete steps on the right and take these (part of Offa's Dyke Path) to descend to the main road. Go straight across through the riverside gardens on the site of the former wharf to reach the car parks near the village hall.

> **– To shorten**
>
> Omit the out-and-back section from Laundry Lane to Newland, saving around 1km (20min) but missing a superb village.

The Cathedral of the Forest

The centrepiece of the attractive village of Newland is the magnificent church, often described as the 'Cathedral of the Forest'. Little remains of the original early 13th-century church but the nave, the long chancel and the porch are all from the first rebuilding around 1300. The tower, with its pinnacles and parapet is a striking centrepiece, while inside there is a famous brass commemorating freemining in the forest. An impressive cross (restored by the Victorians but with old steps) dominates the churchyard.

The Miner's Brass in Newland church

Offa's Dyke Path alongside Harper's Grove

WALK 4
The Kymin from Wyesham

Start/finish	St James' Church, Wyesham
Locate	///directly.maple.dizziness
Cafes/pubs	None on route
Transport	Bus 69 (hourly) from Chepstow and Monmouth
Parking	Roadside parking in Wyesham
Toilets	No public toilets on route

Time 1hr 45min
Distance 5.5km (3.4 miles)
Climb 215m

A little-known but delightful ascent, historic buildings on the Kymin, and superb woodlands

The centrepiece of this exceptional walk is the designed landscape of the Kymin, with its remarkable Georgian buildings on the summit, together with parkland walks developed during the heyday of 'picturesque' tourism in the lower Wye Valley. The climb through Lord's Grove on a medieval trackway and the views on the descent to Beaulieu Wood and Wyesham are equally impressive.

The Round House on the Kymin

SHORT WALKS FOREST OF DEAN

1 From the church walk along Wyesham Road, then turn left, now on **Wyesham Lane**, passing cottages as the lane steepens. Ignore a footpath to the left, staying on the tarmac, now signposted as a bridleway to Redbrook. The tarmac ends at a hairpin bend below **Sky Farm**, just after an attractive modern distance marker.

2 Keep straight ahead here, now on a superb sunken bridleway climbing through the woodland of **Lord's Grove**. The path swings left, steepens and becomes rocky for a while, then the woodland falls away to the left, with views past **Upper Beaulieu Farm** to Bunjups Wood. The path meets Offa's Dyke Path at a kissing gate on the ancient Duffield's Lane.

Contemporary milestone below Sky Farm

The farms at Beaulieu, with their medieval field patterns, were part of the grange of Grace Dieu Abbey,

Wyesham Lane climbing through Lord's Grove

WALK 4 – THE KYMIN FROM WYESHAM

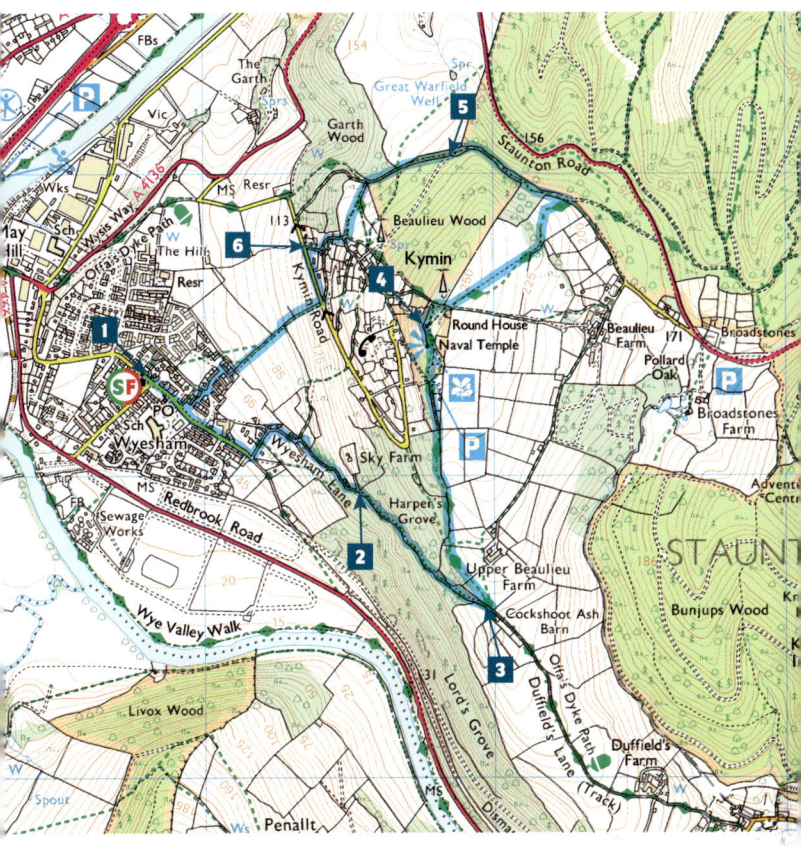

which was in existence in 1226 and remained the landowner until the Dissolution of the Monasteries in the 16th century.

3 Turn left through the kissing gate, keeping close to the left-hand field edge before taking the path on the upper edge of the wooded **Harper's Grove** and crossing a big upland pasture, with increasingly wide views to the right. A narrow path between fences leads across a lane, through a small car park and past the Naval Temple to the **Round House**.

The Naval Temple celebrating Napoleonic War victories

> ⓘ *Dean was designated as a royal hunting forest by the Normans. Forest Law protected the King's beasts, especially deer, which were prized for hunting and venison.*

4 Just beyond the Round House Offa's Dyke Path swings left; turn right here, go through a gate and follow a very well-defined path running diagonally across a field. There are excellent views ahead of Highmeadow Woods beyond a patchwork of fields. Go through a kissing gate at the end of a second field and veer left, following a level track through the Woodland Trust's **Beaulieu Wood**. The track swings left as the woodland falls away to the right, with a footpath signposted to the right.

5 Take the footpath along the woodland edge, descending gently, and go straight on at a junction of paths (there are great views to the right here). Keep straight ahead again at a gate, now briefly back on Offa's Dyke Path, but when the long-distance path goes half-left between fences, cross the right-hand side of a little pasture. Beyond a gate, find a path on the right between hedges, going steeply down a flight of steps and becoming a superb hidden path past cottages down to Kymin Road, a narrow country lane.

WALK 4 – THE KYMIN FROM WYESHAM

6 Turn left along the lane, then climb a stile and drop down steeply along a field edge, with the village of **Wyesham** coming into view below. A kissing gate leads to a clear path between hedges and fences. The prospect over the Wye floodplain to Buckholt Wood and the hills of Monmouthshire is enchanting. Keep straight ahead to find a field gate leading to an alley between houses. Turn right, then left on a minor road and finally right by a little green, with Wyesham Road now straight ahead. Turn right to reach the church.

The treasures of the Kymin

An astonishing and precious survival, the designed parkland on the summit of the Kymin – now cared for by the National Trust – includes the remains of pleasure grounds laid out with circular walks and viewing platforms, but also two extraordinary buildings. Built by the gentlemen of the Monmouth Picnic Club in 1794, the Round House is a circular Georgian banqueting house, while the adjacent Naval Temple was constructed in 1800 to celebrate the naval victories of the Napoleonic wars.

On the descent from the Kymin towards Beaulieu Wood

The dramatic overhang of Near Hearkening Rock

WALK 5
Near Hearkening Rock and the Buckstone

Start/finish	*White Horse pub, Staunton*
Locate	*///trucks.greet.mountain*
Cafes/pubs	*Pub in Staunton*
Transport	*A few buses a day from Monmouth*
Parking	*Limited roadside parking in Staunton*
Toilets	*No public toilets on route*

This spectacular walk – particularly colourful in autumn – is on excellent paths and forest roads as it explores Highmeadow Woods, an area of ancient woodland which plays host to some extraordinary rock scenery, from the long overhanging cliff face of Near Hearkening Rock to the sheer mass of the Suck Stone and the Buckstone, rolled down the hillside by a group of travelling actors from London in 1885 but now back in its rightful place.

Time 2hr 30min
Distance 7.3km (4.5 miles)
Climb 235m

Forest roads and paths through wonderful broadleaved woodland, and an eclectic collection of rock formations and massive boulders

The Buckstone

The village pound at Staunton

1 Take the lane by the pub, turn left at a T-junction and walk past the attractive octagonal village pound to the remains of the medieval cross. Go over the main road and past the church to take the lane at **Whippington's Corner**. Keep straight ahead at a barrier onto a track descending past old iron workings, with coppiced hazel and beech to the left. Keep on the main track to reach a forest crossroads at **Coalpit Hill**.

2 Turn left, following the forest road alongside the **Whippington Brook**, with steep wooded hillsides left and right. A right-hand bend is followed by a long straight stretch, with superb stands of mature beech to the left, until a signpost indicates the Wysis Way crossing the track.

3 Take the Wysis Way to the left, climbing steadily past scowles. These are shallow depressions indicating old opencast iron ore workings. Continue through delightful deciduous woodland to reach a board with information about **Lady Park Wood**. Keep straight ahead, with the high fence protecting the woodland to the right, to reach a second information board.

A national nature reserve, Lady Park Wood is an ancient broadleaved woodland untouched since 1944, a rare example of unmanaged semi-natural woodland.

WALK 5 – NEAR HEARKENING ROCK AND THE BUCKSTONE

4 Turn right here (ignore the path straight ahead) and take the forest road which curves gently to the left. Stay on the forest road until a signpost on the right indicates the Wysis Way and Highmeadow Trail. Take this narrow path through the trees for 100m to find the top of **Near Hearkening Rock** with its spectacular views, then go round to the right to descend steeply to the foot of the rock. A further descent past huge

The massive bulk of the Suck Stone

boulders leads to the **Suck Stone**; turn right above this, then left to drop down to a wide forest track.

5 Turn left along the track, with the Suck Stone now above to the left and outstanding views into Wales, with the Skirrid and Sugar Loaf to the right. The 'holy' Skirrid Mountain is instantly recognisable from its asymmetrical ridge. After 700m take the narrow path on the left, climbing alongside a fence and crossing a stream just below the **Calf Well** to reach and turn right along a level path. Keep straight ahead, through woodland carpeted with bluebells in spring, then drop down slightly to the right and climb past **St John the Baptist's Well** to reach the main road.

6 Cross the road and take the lane rising to the right, but immediately beyond a gate take the footpath running alongside a mossy wall to reach the **Buckstone**, another remarkable rock with terrific views. Once a rocking stone, the Buckstone was dislodged by Victorian vandals and is now cemented in place. Take the green path curving round a covered reservoir, turn left on a metalled lane, zigzag right and left onto another narrow lane, and then turn left to return to the White Horse.

WALK 5 – NEAR HEARKENING ROCK AND THE BUCKSTONE

> **– To shorten**
> Turn left at Waypoint 6 and walk along the main road back to the pub, saving 1.5km (25min).

Near Hearkening Rock and the Suck Stone

The views from above Near Hearkening Rock are stunning, but it's the long overhanging escarpment that takes the breath away. It was once prized by gamekeepers, who used its acoustic qualities to pick up the sounds of poachers in the woods below.

The Suck Stone is widely regarded as the largest detached boulder in Britain. Possibly weighing some 14,000 tonnes, it is an enormous quartz conglomerate block which has slipped downhill from the escarpment above.

Bluebell woods near Staunton

The Wye Valley from Eddy's Lane

WALK 6
Brierley and Ruardean Hill

Time 2hr 30min
Distance 7.7km (4.8 miles)
Climb 180m

Start/finish	Junction of A4136 and Pludds Road, Brierley
Locate	///confined.courtyard.burglars
Cafes/pubs	None on route
Transport	No public transport
Parking	Limited roadside parking in Brierley
Toilets	No public toilets on route

An easy stroll including a beaver enclosure, old mines and disused railway lines, and fabulous views

An exploration of forest tracks and old bridleways in the undulating open country on the northern edge of the Forest, passing a fenced enclosure where beavers have produced young (known as kits) in recent years and going through lanes and wildflower meadows with extensive views to the north into the Wye Valley and Herefordshire. The route then visits mining villages and hamlets and ends with a delightful streamside walk through open woodland.

Looking towards the Welsh hills from Horse Lea

SHORT WALKS FOREST OF DEAN

1 Follow Pludds Road for 400m, then just before the lane bends sharply to the right at Piano Corner go past a metal barrier to find a gravelled track with the **Greathough Brook** to its left. Piano Corner is said to mark the spot where a piano fell off a truck. Secure fencing to the left protects the beaver enclosure. Take the left fork onto a narrower track after 300m, still following the stream, and continue ahead when the beaver enclosure ends, quickly reaching an old railway bridge.

The left turn alongside Greathough Brook

> Beavers were introduced in 2019 to a 6 hectare enclosure along the Greathough Brook, securely protected by a wild boar-proof fence. Evidence of their work constructing dams and lodges can be glimpsed from the path.

2 Scramble up to the left just before the railway bridge and turn right along the old railway line, now a cycle and footpath. The Severn & Wye Railway ran between Lydney and Lydbrook but closed to passenger traffic in 1929. Cross a second bridge, with a clearing to the right, and look out for a crossroads of footpaths 200m beyond a house on the left.

3 Leave the disused railway track here to take the unsignposted but clear path on the right, climbing quite steeply at first. The path swings right and left, joins a broader path and threads its way through brambles and bracken to reach an unsurfaced lane at a hairpin bend. Fork right between cottages to the left and woodland to the right, to reach a T-junction at the top of Timber Tump.

4 Turn left at the junction and in just 50m turn right and follow the metalled lane through the hamlet of **Horse Lea**. Take the obvious path across a little common and turn left onto another quiet lane, which quickly reaches the hamlet of **Readings**. Keep straight ahead between cottages to locate a shady green lane, which eventually emerges onto Eddy's Lane. Cross the

The path between cottages at Readings

WALK 6 – BRIERLEY AND RUARDEAN HILL

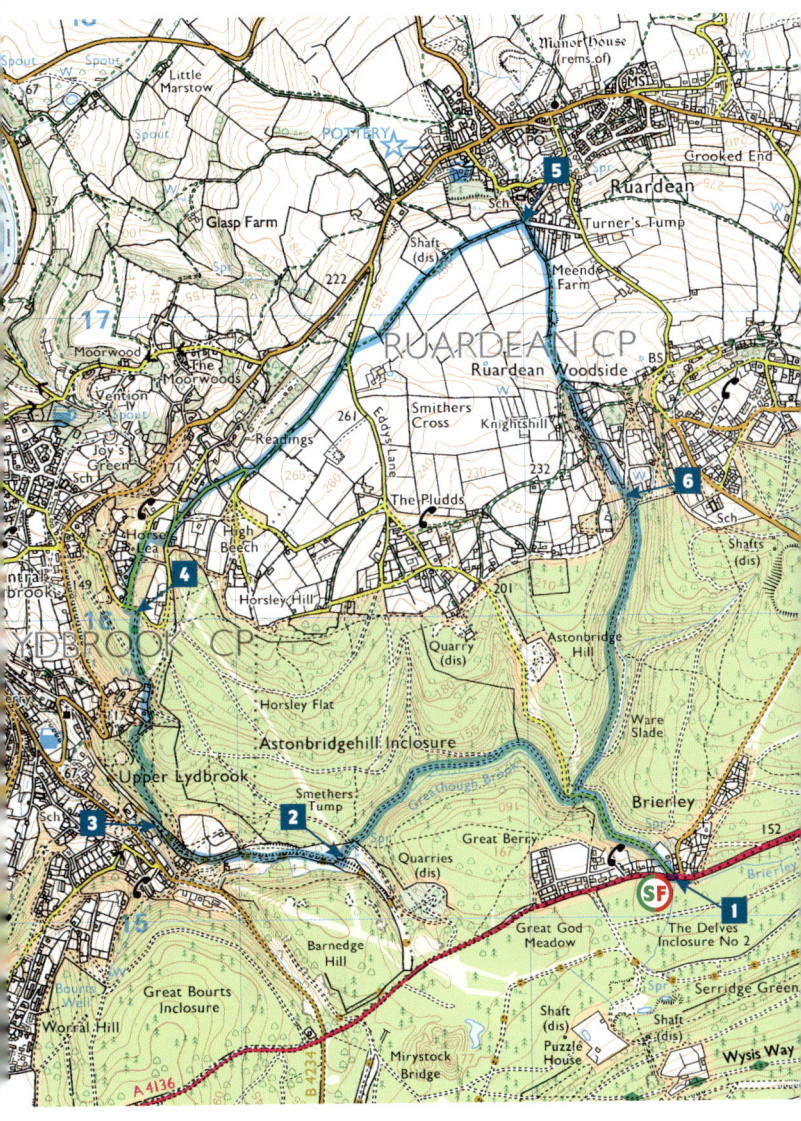

Ruardean village from Turner's Tump

road, go slightly left and then climb a high stile on the right into a superb hay meadow. The path cuts through the meadow, then crosses sheep pastures, finally emerging at a country lane on the edge of **Turner's Tump**.

5 Turn sharp right onto a footpath, which runs alongside a fence, before negotiating a stone stile into open country with the forest ahead. Keep to the right-hand field boundary, passing to the right of an old spoil tip of True Blue Colliery, to reach a stile with stone steps beyond. Cross another field, with the old mining village of **Ruardean Woodside** to the left, to reach a narrow lane. Follow the lane downhill until it swings sharply to the left.

6 Go straight ahead onto a narrow path through bracken (ignore the track further right). The path enters woodland and quickly improves, becoming a delightful path following a stream gently downhill. When a wider track joins from the left, continue down Ware Slade, quickly reaching a forestry barrier at Piano Corner. Turn left here to retrace the outward route to **Brierley**.

> ⓘ *There were still 17 free-mines in the area in 1980 but only a handful cling on, including those at Hopewell (also a museum) and Eddy's Lane near Ruardean.*

Cannop Ponds, looking towards Barnhill Plantation

WALK 7
Bixslade and Cannop

Start/finish	Layby at the southern end of Cannop Ponds
Locate	///ruin.growth.cloud
Cafes/pubs	Cafes at Cannop Cycle Centre and Beechenhurst Lodge
Transport	Bus 24 (every 2hr) from Gloucester to Beechenhurst (Waypoint 6)
Parking	Laybys on B4234 (GL14 4JS)
Toilets	At Cannop Cycle Centre and Beechenhurst Lodge

Time 3hr
Distance 9.4km (5.8 miles)
Climb 200m

An initial climb past freemines, tramroads and historic quarries and level tracks to a pair of picturesque lakes

Remarkably well-preserved tramroads, quarries and a variety of mines, including two of the last freemines to survive, punctuate this walk on forest tracks in the heart of the forest. Deep wooded valleys such as Bixslade and Wimberry Slade, together with the twin lakes at Cannop Ponds, home to mandarin ducks and other wildfowl, provide a scenic backdrop, while Worcester Walk is home to an impressive environmental project.

Male Mandarin duck at Cannop Ponds

SHORT WALKS FOREST OF DEAN

1 Go past the barrier onto a gravelly track, but quickly turn left (signposted 'historic tramroad') to follow the line of the **Bixslade** tramroad towards Mine Train Quarry. The stone sleepers which supported the rails are very evident in places and make route-finding easy. Just before the quarry entrance, detour left along a track to visit the Union Colliery memorial and the Monument Mine. Monument Mine was opened in 1980 and was the first new freemine to be dug for decades.

Woodland walking above Bixhead Quarry

The Union Colliery disaster in 1902 trapped seven miners underground for five days after a sudden influx of water from abandoned workings flooded the mine. Three men were rescued but four lost their lives.

The memorial to the Union Colliery disaster

2 Return to the tramroad, which climbs gently up Bixslade as an obvious path, then widens and arrives at the gravelly access road to Bixhead Quarry. Turn immediately left onto an excellent narrow path through open woodland, ignore a path to the right and then turn right at a crossroads of paths, now following the Beechenhurst Trail to the road.

3 Cross the B4226 onto a tarmac lane leading towards Worcester Lodge, and turn sharply left by a gate giving access to Worcester Walk (also known as the **Lodge Inclosure**), taking a narrow woodland path that skirts the open area of the Walk. At the northwest edge of the Inclosure turn right and walk alongside power lines to reach a forest road. Turn left, following this for 500m to a junction of paths.

WALK 7 – BIXSLADE AND CANNOP

The community-focused Worcester Walk Project aims to enhance the natural environment and includes the creation of an orchard, a wildlife pond and two wildflower meadows. The site was used in World War II as an ammunitions store and as a German prisoner of war camp.

4 Turn right, descending on a stony path to the dry valley of **Wimberry Slade**. Just before another forest road, turn right (again signposted as a historic tramway) to descend the valley, with tramroad sleepers again visible in places. Another of the forest's remaining freemines, the Cannop Drift, lies in the valley to the left of the path. At a complex junction of tracks, turn left and zigzag down to pass to the left of the old Cannop Colliery buildings. Turn right and walk past the cycle centre cafe to the road.

5 Cross the B4234 on a footbridge. Go slightly left to reach and turn right on a cycle track, then quickly go left on a signposted track which leads to the forest centre at Beechenhurst, with its

> ⓘ *Sheep roam extensively in the Forest, where roads are generally unfenced. Foresters who tend them are known locally as 'sheep badgers'.*

> ⓘ *Dean's freeminers earned the right to work coal 'without tax and hindrance' after their support for King Edward I during a siege of Berwick-on-Tweed.*

cafe and waymarked trails. The route runs across the open, grassy picnic area and down to **Speech House Road**.

6 Go right along the road for a few steps, then cross the road, negotiate a stile and follow the forestry track leading south through **Fox Berrys**. Just beyond some coppiced chestnuts dwarfed by tall pines the Gloucestershire Way comes in from the left, but keep straight ahead on the forestry track and then take a right turn to descend and cross a cycle track at the site of Cannop Wharf station.

7 A pleasant path quickly leads from the site of the station to the outflow from the two **Cannop Ponds**. Cross the little bridge here and pass the Forest of Dean Stoneworks to return to the layby. The Cannop Ponds were constructed in 1826 to supply the huge waterwheel at Parkend Ironworks.

WALK 7 – BIXSLADE AND CANNOP

The path to the Cannop Ponds outflow

Threshold is cast from the iron ore mine at Clearwell Caves

WALK 8
The Dean Sculpture Trail

Start/finish	Beechenhurst Lodge visitor centre
Locate	///boxing.skillet.survive
Cafes/pubs	Cafe at Beechenhurst Lodge
Transport	Bus 24 (every 2hr) from Gloucester to Beechenhurst
Parking	Forestry England car park at Beechenhurst Lodge (GL16 7EG, fee payable)
Toilets	At visitor centre

Time 2hr
Distance 6.8km (4.2 miles)
Climb 95m

An extraordinary and enjoyable walk on forest roads, visiting a varied collection of sculptures in woodland

A highly unusual and very rewarding walk, on easy forest tracks punctuated with a succession of fascinating sculptures. Many of them were specially created to reflect forest life and the old industries of the area, and some are designed to decay over time. An informative and inexpensive leaflet available from the cafe provides details of all the sculptures, while the whole trail is very well signposted.

The visitor centre at Beechenhurst

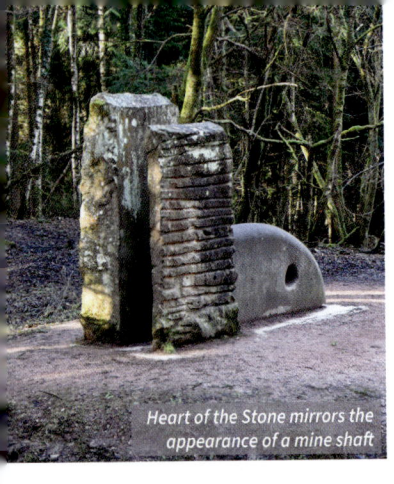
Heart of the Stone mirrors the appearance of a mine shaft

1 Go through the arch marking the beginning of the trail and take the easier route on the left, quickly reaching the first sculpture, *Meander*, which takes its inspiration from the Wye and Severn. Turn left and take a slight detour to see *Heart of the Stone*.

2 Return to the junction of tracks. A long walk along a forest ride eventually brings you to white gates leading onto a cycle trail, with sculptures

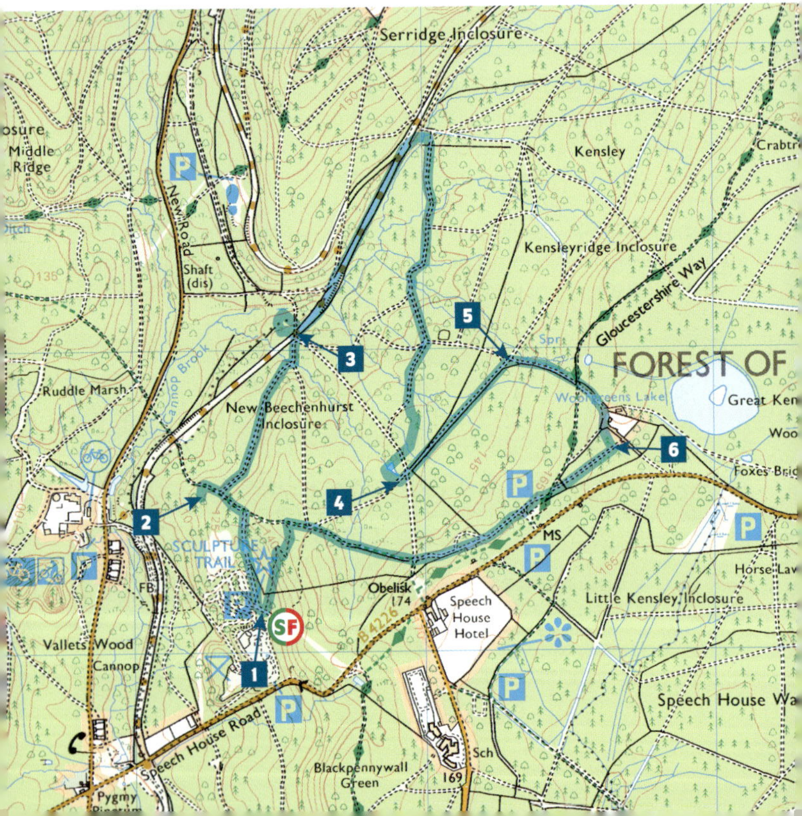

WALK 8 – THE DEAN SCULPTURE TRAIL

including *Fire and Water Boats*, resembling charred canoes, on the far side of the trail.

3 Back at the white gates, follow the trail to one of the oldest and most iconic sculptures, *Iron Road*, installed in 1986 and still evoking the history of railways in the forest. Each sleeper illustrates an aspect of forest life, from charcoal burning and iron smelting to hunting. The path merges with the Colliers Trail, then leaves via a gate on the right, crosses a stream, turns right on a forest road and reaches *Cone and Vessel*, another beautifully carved highlight of the walk. A little further on is *Threshold*, cast from the iron ore mine at Clearwell Caves.

4 Turn left onto another forest road, arriving after around 500m at *Coal Measure Giants*, a sculpture in two parts (the second part is a further 300m along the trail), each with tree fossils and cast-iron sculptures.

5 A right turn and an uphill section leads to *Echo*, a sculpture in front of a miniature quarry, before the trail crosses the Gloucestershire Way, passes to the right of Kensley Lodge with its tall hedges, and reaches probably the most famous of the sculptures, *Cathedral*. Installed in 1986 this sculpture evokes the grandeur of cathedral architecture.

The sleepers of Iron Road illustrate features of forest life

The awe-inspiring sculpture Cathedral

6 Leave *Cathedral* and walk past *Gathering*, representing the fungi of the forest, and through open woodland to drop down to the left on a zig-zagging path back to the visitor centre at Beechenhurst Lodge.

> **— To shorten**
>
> Turn right instead of left at Waypoint 4 and rejoin the trail at the start of the descent to Beechenhurst, saving about 1.8km (25min).

A pioneering sculpture trail

The trail was opened in 1986 and consists of specially selected sculptures reflecting aspects of forest life. New sculptures, commissioned by the Forest of Dean Sculpture Trust, are installed from time to time. Many of the artworks are intended to be ephemeral in nature, in some cases simply dissolving into their surroundings. One of the earliest and best loved of them was *Place*, a massively outsized piece widely known as the giant's chair, which was eventually removed in 2015.

WALK 9
Nagshead Nature Reserve

Start/finish	RSPB Nagshead visitor centre
Locate	///milk.wound.hunk
Cafes/pubs	None on route
Transport	Bus 27 (infrequent service) from Lydney to Parkend (800m from start)
Parking	Small car park at visitor centre (GL15 4LA)
Toilets	In visitor centre (summer weekends only, 11am–3pm)

Time 1hr 45min
Distance 6km (3.7 miles)
Climb 130m

A long but easy climb through a popular nature reserve with excellent birdwatching, returning along forest roads past mines and quarries

The RSPB's Nagshead Nature Reserve is an oasis of tranquillity. This scenic walk explores the reserve, which mostly consists of oak woodland first planted in the early 19th century, a particularly important habitat for pied flycatchers. Other species that can be seen here include great spotted woodpeckers and crossbills. The gentle ascent of Cleave Hill is a real highlight. There is an option to extend the walk to visit the extensive remains of a historic ironworks.

The track passing old collieries near Fetter Hill

SHORT WALKS FOREST OF DEAN

1 Go through the gate to the right of the visitor centre, fork left on an excellent track when the Gloucestershire Way goes off to the right, then keep straight ahead when a trail leaves to the left. In 1942 the Forestry Commission installed 84 nestboxes at Nagshead to encourage tits to breed there, but 15 boxes were occupied by pied flycatchers.

2 The way ahead is very clear, steadily climbing the wooded slopes of **Cleave Hill** on an excellent straight path through mature broadleaved woodland. Eventually the path swings sharply left just after a seat, now with a view of Bixslade (Walk 7) down to the right. Keep straight ahead, climbing gently and crossing a forest road, to reach **Nagshead Lodge**. This was built in 1810 as one of the original Forest lodges.

3 Go past a barrier and immediately turn left onto the first of two paths. Keep straight on beneath power lines and then through a stretch of coniferous woodland, still on a good path which follows the edge of the forest,

Classic deciduous woodland on Cleave Hill

WALK 9 – NAGSHEAD NATURE RESERVE

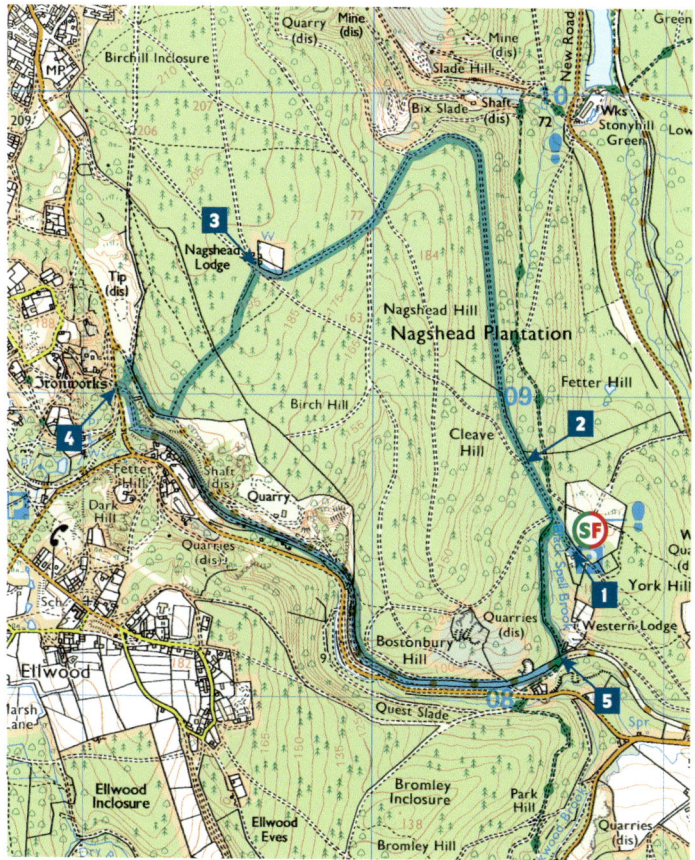

with heathland on the right, and drops down to meet a gravel quarry access road. Turn right here, then left after 150m onto a narrow path which descends to meet a shared-use track at the point where it crosses a road.

4 Turn left to follow the shared path past the remains of collieries and a quarry. The path is tracing the line of the Severn & Wye Railway's Coleford branch, which served stone quarries, collieries and iron mines.

The capped shaft of Hopewell Engine colliery

Darkhill Ironworks

The remains of Hopewell Engine colliery lie to the right of the track, with the circular shaft very prominent. Point Quarry worked Pennant sandstone, and the original tramroad from the quarry passed under the railway in a short tunnel.

The wide gravelly track slices through a rock cutting below **Bostonbury Hill** to reach a tarmac lane.

5 Turn left here, passing the entrance to **Western Lodge** and taking the Gloucestershire Way past a barrier and along a delightful woodland path to a gate. Turn right to retrace the outward route from here, quickly reaching a second gate and swinging right to the visitor centre.

− To shorten

Fork left at Waypoint 2 and follow the trail directly to Nagshead Lodge, saving 0.9km (20min).

+ To lengthen

To visit the Darkhill Ironworks, cross the road at Waypoint 4 and follow the cycle track to a memorial to metallurgist David Mushet, who perfected a steel-making technique here. Allow at least 30min to explore the site.

Woorgreens Lake and Kensleyridge Inclosure

WALK 10
Crabtree Hill and Woorgreens Lake

Time 1hr 30min
Distance 4.5km (2.8 miles)
Climb 50m

Easy walking across delightful open heathland in the centre of the Forest

Start/finish	Speech House Woodlands
Locate	///unopposed.boomed.emotional
Cafes/pubs	None on route. Pub 300m west of start
Transport	Bus 24 (every 2hr) from Gloucester to Speech House (300m from start)
Parking	Speech House Woodlands car park (GL16 7EH)
Toilets	No public toilets on route

An easy walk through open and sandy lowland heath in the heart of the Forest, with Woorgreens Lake just to the south. The contrast with the surrounding woodland is spectacular, and the wildlife includes fallow deer and a variety of bird species – there is every chance (especially around dawn and dusk) of seeing and hearing the nightjar, with its unique churring song.

The path onto the heath

1 Take the path at the north-eastern corner of the car park and swing round to the left, ignoring a sculpture trail signpost and following a wide path through bracken. Keep straight ahead at a crossroads of paths, now on a wider track with a muddy pond down to the right. After 600m go through a gate just beyond an information board, with livestock holding pens just to the right.

> The open sandy heath on Crabtree Hill is at the centre of an ambitious restoration project, which is using cattle and ponies to control the vegetation and improve the nature conservation value of the site.

2 Keep straight on, now on a narrower path between the trees of **Kensleyridge Inclosure** at first and then across open sandy heathland. Notices warn of the presence of ground-nesting birds here, including the rare nightjar, and request that dogs are kept on leads. Pass a seat on the left, then after 20m fork right onto a delightful grassy path. Turn right on reaching the far side of the heath, now on a well-used path which quickly reaches a complex junction of tracks and paths on the modest summit of **Crabtree Hill**. A cast-iron sign to the right commemorates the re-enclosure of the area in 1896.

Conservation grazing with Highland cattle near the holding pens

WALK 10 – CRABTREE HILL AND WOORGREENS LAKE

The right fork across the heath

3 Go slightly right across a wide metalled forestry road and take the grassy track heading south-east across the heath, passing a single oak and then a stand of venerable beech trees. Go through a gate and after 50m turn right at a T-junction onto a rutted track. The track becomes roughly surfaced and reaches another gate, with a cattle trough beyond and to the right.

4 Head to the left of the cattle trough, now on a gravelled road with **Great Kensley Inclosure** to the left, but after 300m look carefully for a

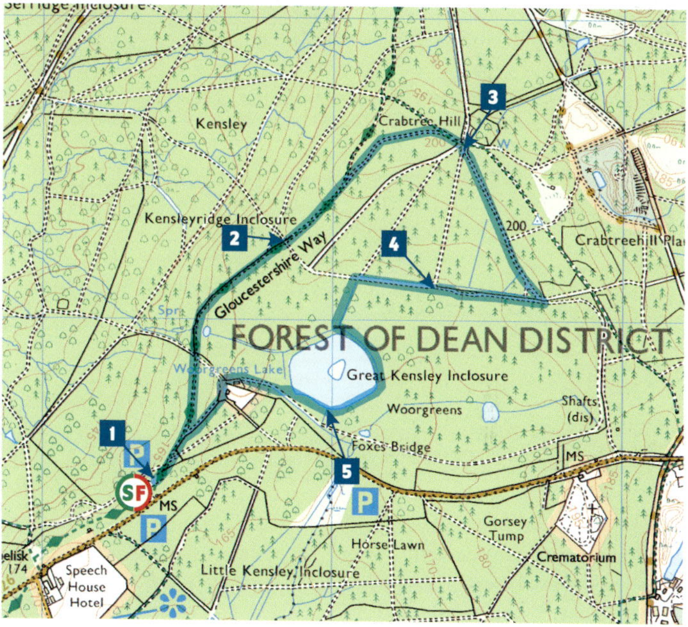

The heath from the cast-iron re-enclosure sign

grassy path to the left (it is signposted with a low waymark post). The path runs through a grove of alders, and is uneven and sometimes boggy after rain. Go through a gate and turn left to skirt **Woorgreens Lake** on a narrow path, with side paths leading to the lake shore. Cross a footbridge and swing right for a second bridge to arrive at the lake's outlet at a dog-splash area.

> **Woorgreens Lake, a large shallow lake on the site of an opencast coal mine, attracts hobbies hawking for dragonflies in summer, and in winter is an important site for goosanders, grebes and geese.**

5 Follow the lakeshore for a further 150m then turn left on a clear path and immediately turn right (don't go through the gate straight ahead) to walk through the trees, passing to the right of a series of wooden sheds. Turn left on a wide track, with Kensley Lodge – one of the original forest lodges – on the left, then go right, following sculpture trail signposts, to rejoin the outward route and quickly return to the car park.

WALK 11
Soudley Valley Rural Geology Trail

Start/finish	Soudley Village Hall
Locate	///overture.steadily.satellite
Cafes/pubs	Pub in Soudley
Transport	Bus 72 (every 2hr) from Chepstow and Lydney
Parking	Village hall car park (GL14 2TZ)
Toilets	At village hall

Time 1hr 30min
Distance 4.4km (2.7 miles)
Climb 140m

Follow forest tracks to explore 100 million years of Earth's geological history

Geologists will enjoy the exposures of Devonian sandstones, Carboniferous limestones and coal measures along this trail, but there are also rich pickings for landscape enthusiasts and those interested in industrial history. Shallow iron workings dating from the Iron Age, evidence of coal mining, railway relics and quarrying and brickmaking are all present in this compact valley, while two iconic sculptures help interpret the area's past.

The path through the upper level of Blue Rock quarry

SHORT WALKS FOREST OF DEAN

1 Walk back across the car park access bridge to the main road, turning left along Upper Road to reach the start of the trail as it makes its way through a cutting on the former Bullo Pill to Cinderford railway. The Old Red Sandstones exposed here, deposited around 370 million years ago, are the oldest rocks encountered on the trail. Follow the old railway track to an open area, once the site of Soudley furnace, with the bricked-up entrance to the Blue Rock tunnel beyond.

The start of the geology trail

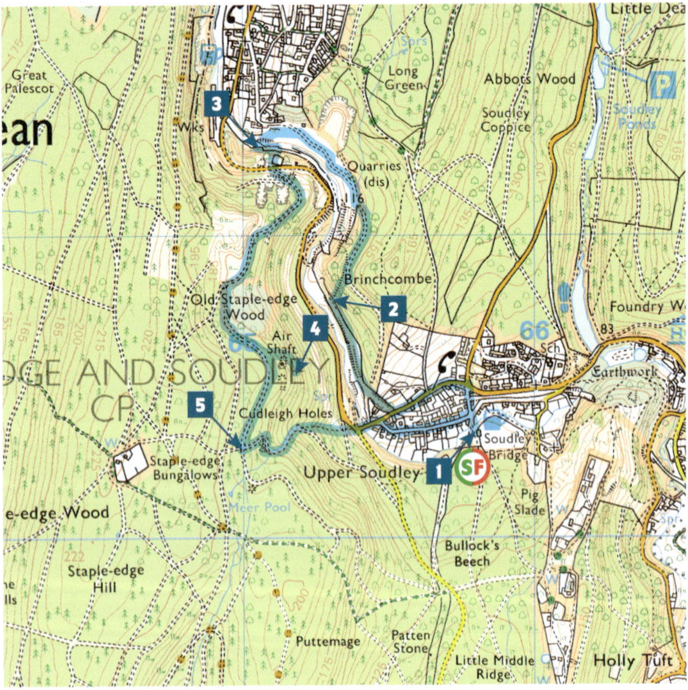

The loading ramp at Shakemantle Quarry

To the right of the Blue Rock tunnel the impressive statue *Nearly There* commemorates the last days of the local coal industry. Steps on the left used to lead to the *Hod Boy* sculpture but this has now been moved to the Dean Heritage Centre (Walk 12).

2 Go back 30m from the tunnel entrance to find the narrow path leading uphill and climb stone steps leading into a rock cutting at the top of the Blue Rock limestone quarry, and then follow a level path well above the valley bottom to arrive at the massive Shakemantle Quarry, with its loading ramp still in place. A little further on is

The Nearly There sculpture near Blue Rock tunnel

the brickworks which used lime dust from the quarry as raw material. Bear left beyond the brickworks to drop down and rejoin the old railway track.

3 Turn left along the track, cross a bridge and after 40m take a narrow path rising to the right to cross a road. Climb past a barrier on a good track which skirts the Shakemantle sand quarries. Birds of prey such as buzzards and goshawks, whose warning cries reverberate around the hillsides, are common here. As the track bends right, take the left-hand of two paths going off to the left, initially as a narrow path through **Old Staple-edge Wood** but later becoming a green and marshy track. A path on the left leads to the tall Findall Chimney.

Findall Chimney was built in the 18th century to provide ventilation to the iron mine over which it was constructed. A fire set in the chimney drew foul air from the mine and replaced it with clean air.

Findall Chimney

4 Return to the main path and turn left. The trees fall back on the left, with a superb stretch of easy walking on a wide green path, until, just before a fenced enclosure on the right, a decent path descends gently to the left.

5 The path meanders down towards the Soudley valley, passing ancient ironstone workings (the shallow drifts known as scowles) and veering sharply to the left. When the path goes sharp right, continue ahead on a rough path, negotiating rocks and fallen branches to emerge at a road junction. Continue ahead, then turn right onto Lower Road to return to the village hall.

The wide green track south of Old Staple-edge Wood

WALK 12
Blaize Bailey from Soudley Ponds

Time 1hr 45min
Distance 4.7km (2.9 miles)
Climb 130m

Start/finish	Soudley Ponds
Locate	///lyricist.press.cosmetic
Cafes/pubs	Cafe at Dean Heritage Centre, pub in Upper Soudley
Transport	Bus 72 (every 2hr) from Chepstow to heritage centre (Waypoint 5)
Parking	Soudley Ponds car park (GL14 2TX)
Toilets	No public toilets on route

Wildlife ponds, exhilarating woodland walking, a renowned viewpoint, and a fascinating heritage museum

While this is a short walk it is richly rewarding, including the three ponds in the Soudley valley, now a nature reserve, and the well-known viewpoint at Blaize Bailey, overlooking the horseshoe bends of the River Severn with the long ridge of the Cotswold hills behind. A splendid museum in the former Camp Mill adds even greater variety to the walk.

Blaize Bailey viewpoint

SHORT WALKS FOREST OF DEAN

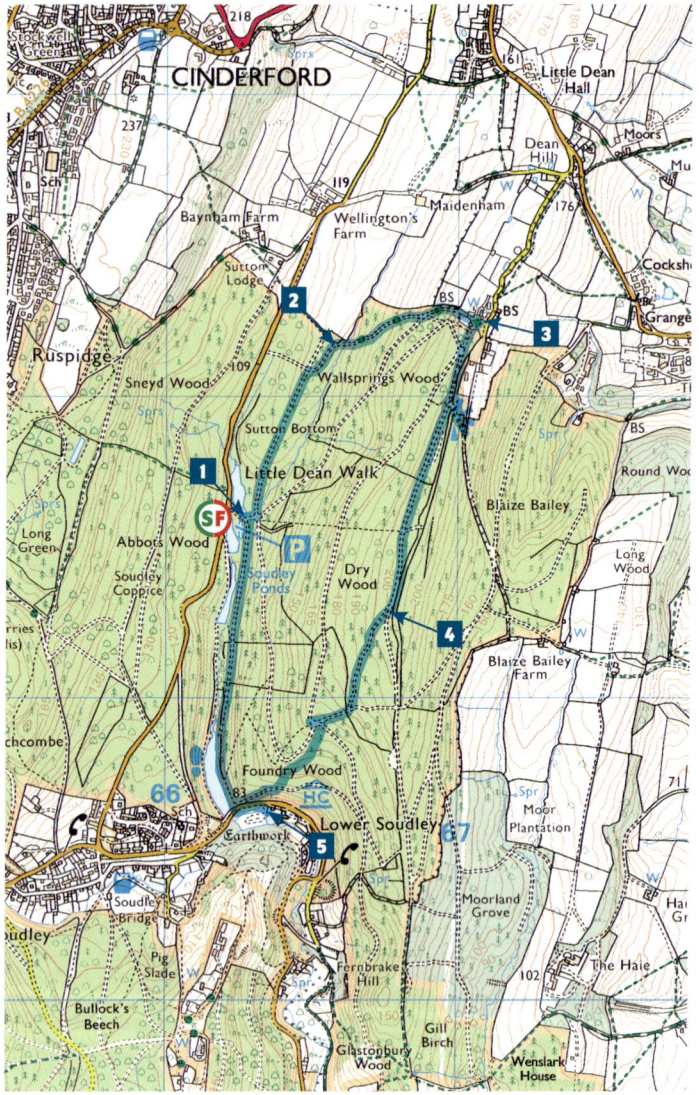

WALK 12 – BLAIZE BAILEY FROM SOUDLEY PONDS

1 Take the left-hand forest road, going past a barrier and climbing gently through mature woodland. Just before the forest edge fork right onto a track, which narrows into a good footpath and reaches a junction with a view of fields ahead.

2 Turn right, still just inside the forest, and drop down to cross a little stream before climbing through **Wallsprings Wood**. Views from the edge of the forest are of Wellington's Farm and the pastures around Littledean. The path climbs past a cottage and reaches a tarmac lane on the crest of the most easterly ridge in the Forest, with sudden views down to and across the Severn.

Walking past Blaize Bailey Cottage

The Severn plain from Blaize Bailey

3 Turn right on the lane, walk immediately to the left of Blaize Bailey Cottage, fork left on a forest road and left again at a curious 'roundabout' to reach the superb Blaize Bailey **viewpoint**.

> ⓘ *Pioneering DJ Jimmy Young, whose Radio 2 programme ran for 30 years, was born at Cinderford in the heart of the Forest.*

The highlight of the panorama from the Blaize Bailey viewpoint is the great horseshoe bend of the meandering River Severn around the Arlingham peninsula, with Gloucester and the Cotswold scarp providing a stunning backdrop.

Return to the roundabout and turn left on a forest road running through an open landscape until the track swings left after 750m.

4 Go to the right here on a narrow path through **Dry Wood**, with the edge of a conifer plantation to the right and younger mixed woodland to the left. The way bends right, then at a complex junction turn left and almost immediately right on a clear forest footpath (not marked on the OS map). This descends steadily through **Foundry Wood**, veers right onto a more substantial path and emerges at the lowest of the Soudley Ponds. The Dean Heritage Centre lies 100m along the road to the left.

5 Return to the pond and take the obvious path alongside the water, gaining height almost imperceptibly

The working waterwheel at Dean Heritage Centre

through the nature reserve. An easy walk alongside the upper pond quickly arrives back at the car park.

The ponds, which were originally constructed to provide power for a foundry lower down the valley, are now home to wildfowl and dragonflies, with little grebe and mandarin ducks both resident, the latter nesting in the lower branches of overhanging trees.

Dean Heritage Centre

Dean Heritage Centre, housed in the former Camp Mill

The heritage centre museum traces aspects of the area's history and development, including the Yorkley hoard of Roman coins discovered in 2012 and displays illustrating the social and cultural history of the Forest. There are outside displays such as a forester's cottage, a cider press and a striking waterwheel. Housed in the former Camp Mill, which utilised water power from the Soudley Ponds, the centre also has a shop and cafe.

Ponies grazing on the summit plateau

WALK 13
May Hill

Start/finish	Glasshouse
Locate	///conductor.blown.tiredness
Cafes/pubs	Pub at Glasshouse (restricted opening hours)
Transport	No public transport
Parking	Roadside parking immediately north of the pub
Toilets	No public toilets on route

Time 3hr
Distance 8km (5 miles)
Climb 240m

A simple climb to an iconic summit with an astonishing panorama, followed by an old cider house and a peaceful woodland walk

Instantly recognisable from many directions, May Hill is a much-loved local landmark and is easily climbed on excellent tracks. The summit is crowned with a distinctive group of pine trees planted in 1887 to commemorate the golden jubilee of Queen Victoria, while a low ditch surrounding the summit possibly dates from the Iron Age. Conservation grazing is improving biodiversity, with wild daffodils, bluebells and heath bedstraw all thriving.

The northern scarp of the Forest from May Hill

1 Take the broad track (signposted Wysis Way) at the side of the pub, keep straight on when it narrows to a path, fork left after just 5m and continue ahead when the Wysis Way peels off to the left. Cross a stream and turn right at a signpost onto an excellent path which climbs steadily on the edge of **Castle Hill Wood**. The path meets a gravelly track; turn right here then follow a sometimes muddy lane to a minor road. Turn right, soon passing a chapel and reaching the village hall.

2 Take the lane opposite the hall, passing **View Farm** to reach a second road, with a disused chapel on the corner. Go straight across, then fork right onto a minor road climbing past a house called The Nook. The tarmac ends at an open area with a variety of paths and tracks.

3 Turn sharply left, now back on the Wysis Way, onto a track between tall hedges. The Gloucestershire Way comes in from the left, then the way lies straight on, through an informal parking area, eventually emerging through a gate onto the open higher slopes of **May Hill**. The summit, with its distinctive clump of trees encircled

The ditch encircling May Hill's summit

WALK 13 – MAY HILL

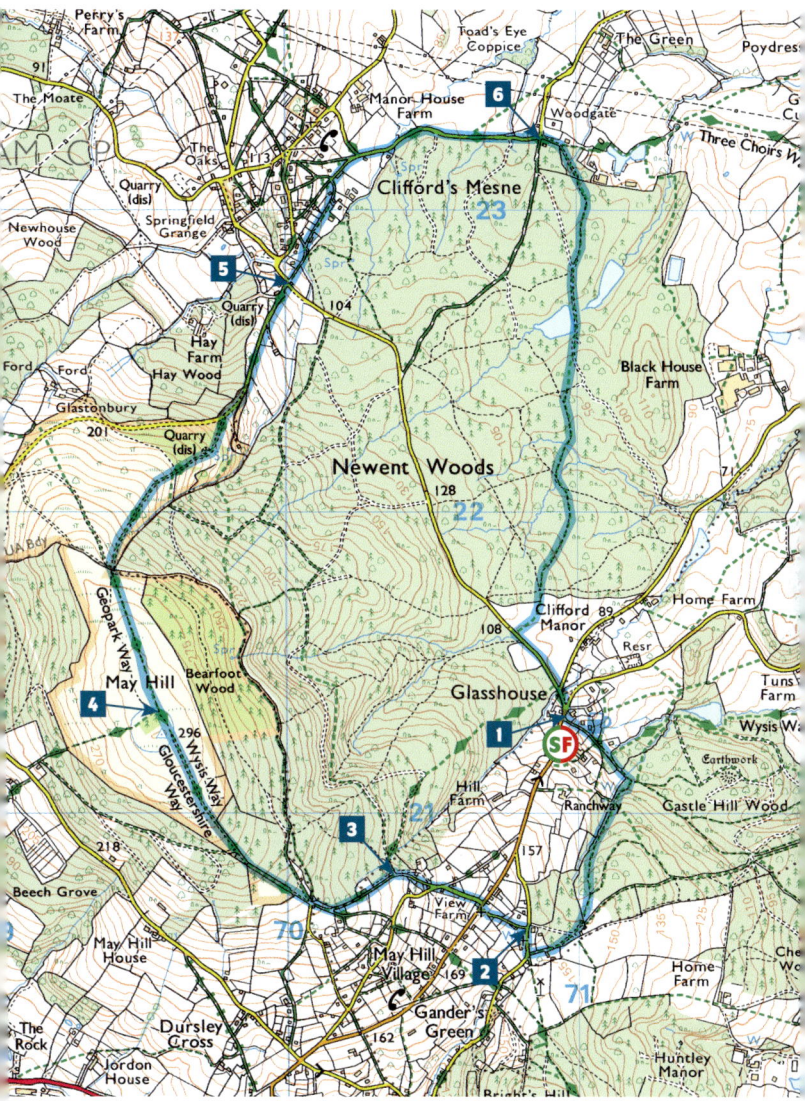

79

> ⓘ *Fallow deer, reintroduced into Dean in the 1940s, now number several hundred and are especially common in the central wooded areas.*

by an ancient, shallow ditch, stands at a mere 296m and so is easily reached across open grassland.

May Hill is especially popular on May Day, with many walkers aiming to be at the summit at sunrise and Morris dancers providing entertainment, followed by breakfast in the village hall.

4 Carry on across the grassy plateau, with a gentle descent well to the right of a lone hawthorn tree. The grass is close-cropped from conservation grazing using ponies and Belted Galloway cattle. Go through a gate and take the right-hand option, now on a stony track which drops down through woodland to reach a country lane. Turn right to arrive in **Clifford's Mesne** by the (closed) Yew Tree Inn, once a well-known cider house.

5 Go straight across a road and follow a footpath on the edge of the village, crossing a stream on a footbridge and keeping right on a path which reaches a little common and then a surfaced lane. Follow the lane round to the right, passing Lower Farm and an attractive cottage, with woodland to the right and an open fieldscape on the left, until the road bends sharply left.

6 Go straight ahead (signposted Three Choirs Way) through the entrance gates to Woodgate Farm, but turn right after only 100m onto a track heading through **Newent Woods**, a detached fragment of the Forest of Dean. The birdlife here includes redstart, lesser redpoll and spotted flycatcher. The route is straightforward, passing between the Huntley Pools, taking a right fork, crossing two streams and climbing a stile at the edge of the wood. Go straight on across a field, with **Clifford Manor** away to the left, and turn left on the road to arrive back at Glasshouse Green.

> ⓘ *The rocks of May Hill range from hard limestones to soft sandstones. The oldest, hardest rocks have been folded into a dome rising above the softer sandstones on the lower slopes of the hill.*

Newent Woods and Clifford Manor

– To shorten

From the start take the Clifford's Mesne road for 100m, turn left onto Wysis Way and climb the broad track to Waypoint 3. This saves 0.5km (10min) but the track is rutted and can be very muddy.

The May Hill panorama

The summit of May Hill boasts almost a 360-degree panorama, with the Cotswolds and the Malvern Hills to the north and east, much of southern Herefordshire in sight to the north-west, with the Radnor Hills beyond, the scarp of the Black Mountains and the Brecon Beacons distantly to the west, and the eastern ridges of the Forest of Dean closer at hand to the south.

Tibbscross Farm and Green Bottom

WALK 14
St Anthony's Well and Welshbury Hill

Start/finish	*Gunn's Mill near Mitcheldean*
Locate	*///sparkles.frames.interrupt*
Cafes/pubs	*None on route*
Transport	*No public transport*
Parking	*Limited roadside parking*
Toilets	*No public toilets on route*

A classic walk in east Dean, from one of the best preserved early blast furnaces in northern Europe to a stone-built well with a remarkable history, a hidden hill fort on Welshbury Hill and a former Cistercian abbey at Flaxley. There are impressive woodlands and superb views across the Severn Estuary to the Cotswolds from the high pastures between Welshbury Wood and Chestnuts Inclosure.

Time 1hr 45min
Distance 5.3km (3.3 miles)
Climb 140m

Woodland tracks and open paths across farmland, with spectacular views across the Severn and an ancient healing well

St Anthony's Well

SHORT WALKS FOREST OF DEAN

1 Head up Lower Spout Lane past the contrasting sights of Gunn's Mill and the Asha Centre, keeping to the sometimes muddy lane past a house with camping facilities. When the track bends right, take a path climbing diagonally to the left.

2 The diagonal path quickly leads to the extraordinary sight of **St Anthony's Well** in a small woodland valley.

St Anthony's Well, last restored in the late 18th century, was in use in Iron Age, Roman and medieval times. Its water runs through a bathing pool which was used for baptisms in the 19th century. Long used for healing purposes, its water is said to cure skin diseases.

Beyond the well a path climbs steeply to reach a good level track;

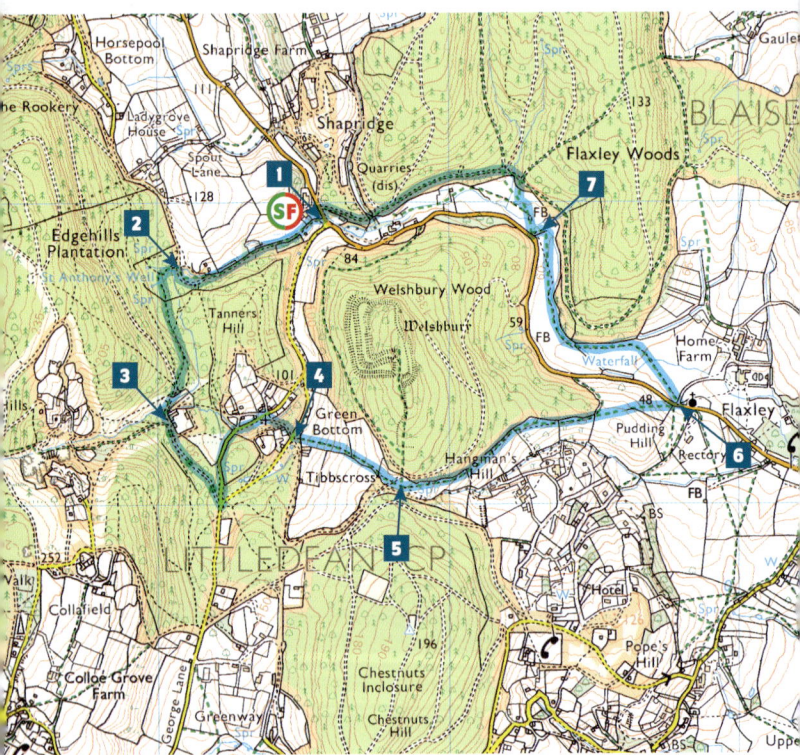

Crossing Pudding Hill

turn left here to reach and turn left at a forest road. Go through a barrier to reach a minor lane at the edge of the hamlet of Green Bottom.

3 Fork left to follow the road past the old East Dean Waterworks buildings. The road leads down to a junction; turn sharp left onto the lane which leads into the centre of **Green Bottom**, with Beulah Chapel at its heart. The chapel was opened in 1877 as a Baptist preaching station. Take the narrow path to the left of the chapel, passing a house and dropping down on a concreted drive to reach and cross the road at **Tibbscross**.

4 The path lies slightly to the left, across a stile, but can be swamped by vegetation in summer, when a diversion through the farmyard may be preferable. Climb steeply up the hill, keeping to the right-hand fenceline, to reach the narrow open plateau between **Welshbury Wood** and **Chestnuts Inclosure**.

5 Keep to the edge of Welshbury Wood, passing through several fields above **Hangman's Hill**. The views across the River Severn towards the Cotswolds are superb. Beyond a kissing gate the path crosses an enormous field on Pudding Hill, gradually losing

The view east from the plateau by Chestnuts Inclosure

height, to a stile giving access to the road opposite the parish church at **Flaxley**, with Flaxley Abbey beyond.

> Flaxley was founded as a Cistercian monastery in 1143 on the spot where the Earl of Hereford fell while hunting. After the Dissolution of the Monasteries by Henry VIII it was given to Sir William Kingston, overseer of the execution of Anne Boleyn.

> ⓘ *The Forest is a popular location for films and TV, with scenes from* Star Wars, Harry Potter *and* Dr Who *shot at Puzzlewood near Coleford.*

6 Go through the kissing gate to the left of the church and head diagonally across a field, then veer left through a second field to find a wooden footbridge. Turn right, following the right-hand side of a narrow and very long field to reach and turn left on a little lane by Lower Stream Cottage.

7 After 50m turn right through a kissing gate and follow the path across a short causeway and over the stream again, then turn left to follow a clear path through rough pasture. Turn right before a footbridge, climb a stile and take a short narrow path to join a forest road. Turn left and follow this until it reaches the road just beyond Gunn's Mill.

+ To lengthen

At Waypoint 5 go left over a stile in Welshbury Wood to visit the impressive earthworks of Welshbury hill fort, with three ramparts and ditches. This adds 1.5km (30min) to the walk.

Gunn's Mill

Gunn's Mill, currently being painstakingly restored, is the most complete early charcoal-fired blast furnace in Europe. It was operating by 1629 but was destroyed by Commonwealth troops in 1650 and rebuilt in 1683. It was a paper mill by the middle of the 18th century. The remains include the furnace tower, bellows room, casting floor and wheel pit. The adjacent Asha Centre houses a charity working for sustainable development and world peace.

Looking down Newnham High Street to the clock tower

WALK 15
Newnham and Haie Hill

Start/finish	*Clock tower, Newnham High Street*
Locate	*///lamenting.writers.nurses*
Cafes/pubs	*Good selection in Newnham*
Transport	*Bus 23 (hourly) from Gloucester*
Parking	*Roadside parking in Newnham*
Toilets	*At north end of village, 300m from clock tower*

Time 2hr 30min
Distance 8.6km (5.3 miles)
Climb 200m

An attractive village, an old river port, tracks above a historic railway tunnel and stunning river views

The focal point of this walk is the lovely riverside village of Newnham, site of a Roman ford and then of a ferry, which ran from the 13th century for 700 years. It also includes the former river port of Bullo Pill, the notable Haie Hill railway tunnel and a scenic descent from Blaize Bailey farm, with panoramic views across the Severn valley and along the hills of eastern Dean.

Looking back along the Severn to Collow Pill and Newnham church

SHORT WALKS FOREST OF DEAN

1 Start at the clock tower in **Newnham** and walk south along the braided Lower High Street, which runs uphill beneath lime trees to the church. Turn left midway up the hill, onto Severn Street, walking towards the site of the former ferry across the Severn. Turn right up Church Street, then left to cut through the churchyard. There is a magnificent outlook over the Severn, with its great banks of sand at low tide.

2 Turn left on a tarmac path alongside the main road but quickly left again onto a footpath (signposted Severn Way) with a huge red buoy alongside. Go through a kissing gate and follow the path through a long narrow field and on a splendid woodland path, with the Severn below to the left. Finally, the arrow-straight path leads between a fence and a hedge to **Bullo Pill**.

The prominent red buoy above Collow Pill

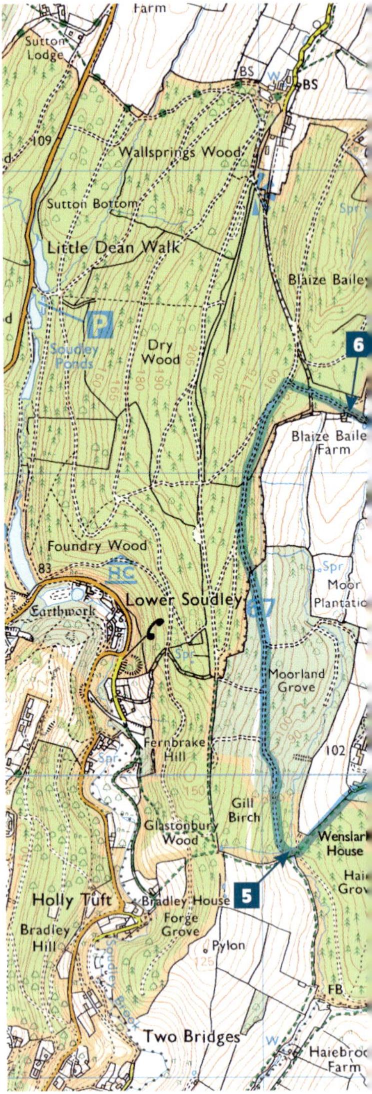

WALK 15 – NEWNHAM AND HAIE HILL

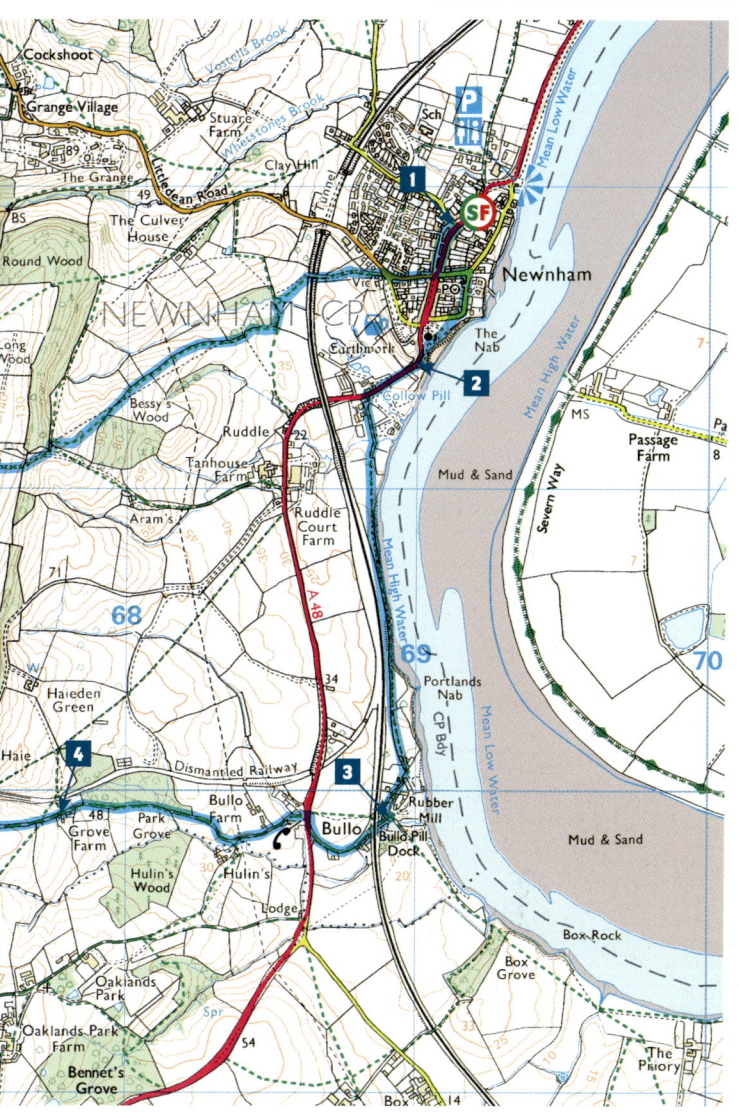

91

The Haie seen above trees that mark the line of the Bullo Pill Railway

WALK 15 – NEWNHAM AND HAIE HILL

The lock gates and dock walls of Bullo Pill, a small tidal creek, still survive but the port has not operated commercially for many years, and the associated industrial development, including a marble works and a rubber mill, has long gone.

> ⓘ *The Severn Bore, a dramatic tidal surge in the Severn Estuary, is especially popular with surfers and is often viewed from Newnham.*

3 Take the lane up to the main road and go diagonally across to find a bridleway which runs between tall hedges past Hulins Farm. Eventually the trees fall back and there is a striking view of **Grove Farm** ahead. Look right on arriving at Grove Farm to see the heavily wooded course of the old railway in a deep cutting as it approaches the Haie Hill tunnel.

The Bullo Pill Railway, originally a horse-drawn tramroad built to export products from the Forest, included the extraordinary Haie Hill tunnel – at 990m it was the longest in the world when it was completed in 1810.

4 Beyond Grove Farm the bridleway becomes an impassable holloway, but go through a gate to the right to walk parallel to the ancient route up into

Grove Farm and the track towards the Blaize Bailey ridge

Long Wood and the ridge leading towards May Hill

woodland, where a shady path beneath rhododendrons leads to the rear access lane to The Haie, a pink-painted Victorian country mansion. Keep straight on here until a field appears straight ahead. Turn left and follow the path along the woodland edge to a timber-stacking area.

5 Go sharply to the right on a broad forest road which climbs steadily. At the top of the hill another forest road joins from the left, then 150m after a green track does the same, turn right on an unsigned but obvious narrow path which reaches the edge of the wood by the forlorn ruins of **Blaize Bailey Farm**.

6 Cross a hayfield and swing right by a barn, then immediately left on a narrow green path. Aim for a stile straight ahead and drop down to curve left around the edge of **Long Wood** to a redundant stile. Take the path going diagonally right to a stile at the left-hand corner of **Bessy's Wood**, then keep to the left edge of successive fields, at first on a stony track. Leave this when it bends right, negotiating two stiles and then crossing the mainline railway. A clear track now reaches **Newnham**; turn right to reach the main road and then left to descend the delightful High Street to the clock tower. The grassy bank in the middle of the street conceals the foundations of two rows of houses.

USEFUL INFORMATION

Trains

Stations at Chepstow, Lydney and Gloucester provide connections to local bus services.

www.crosscountrytrains.co.uk
www.tfw.wales

Buses

Three services run from Gloucester to Coleford, via Cinderford and Ruardean (route 22), Newnham and Lydney (route 23) and Speech House and Cannop (route 24). There are also services from Chepstow to Monmouth via Brockweir and Redbrook (route 69) and Chepstow to Cinderford via Lydney and Soudley (route 72).

www.bustimes.org
www.newportbus.co.uk
www.stagecoachbus.com

Tourism and nature bodies

Forest of Dean and Wye Valley Tourism
www.visitdeanwye.co.uk

Dean Heritage Centre
www.deanheritagecentre.org

RSPB
www.rspb.org.uk

Forestry England – West
tel 0300 067 4800

Tourist information centres

Chepstow
tel 01291 623772

Coleford
tel 01594 837135

Old Station, Tintern
tel 01291 689566

© Mike Dunn 2025
First edition 2025
ISBN: 978 1 78631 288 4
eISBN: 978 1 78765 232 3

Printed in Singapore by KHL Printing using responsibly sourced paper.
A catalogue record for this book is available from the British Library.
All photographs are by Chris and Mike Dunn.
Cover illustration of bluebells in the Forest of Dean by Clare Crooke.

© Crown copyright and database rights 2025 OS AC0000810376

Cicerone's EU representative for GPSR compliance is Easy Access System Europe, Mustamäe tee 50, 10621 Tallinn, Estonia. Email gpsr.requests@easproject.com.

CICERONE

Cicerone Press, Juniper House, Murley Moss, Oxenholme Road,
Kendal, Cumbria, LA9 7RL

www.cicerone.co.uk

Updates to this Guide

While every effort is made to ensure the accuracy of guidebooks as they go to print, changes can occur during the lifetime of an edition. Any updates that we know of for this guide will be on the Cicerone website (www.cicerone.co.uk/1288/updates), so please check before planning your trip. We also advise that you check information about transport, accommodation and shops locally. Even rights of way can be altered over time. We are always grateful for information about any discrepancies between a guidebook and the facts on the ground, sent by email to updates@cicerone.co.uk.

Register your book: To sign up to receive free updates, special offers and GPX files where available, create a Cicerone account and register your purchase via the 'My Account' tab at www.cicerone.co.uk.